Best wishes

The **Arcadia Guide** to MBD and its **elimination** in captivity

www.arcadia-reptile.com

The **Arcadia Guide** to MBD and its **elimination** in captivity

Copyright: John Courteney-Smith
Published: Feb 2013
ISBN: 978-0-9576570-0-7

Publisher: Arcadia Products PLC

The right of John Courteney-Smith to be identified as author of this work has been asserted by him in accordance with sections 77 and 78 of the Copyright, Designs and Patents Act 1988.

All rights reserved. No part of this publication may be reproduced, stored in retrieval system, copied in any form or by any means, electronic, mechanical, photocopying, recording or otherwise transmitted without written permission from the publisher. You must not circulate this book in any format.

For more information see www.arcadia-reptile.com

The **Arcadia Guide** to MBD and its **elimination** in captivity

CONTENTS

Contents	5
Foreword	7
MBD and its Effects Upon Captive Reptiles	11
Diet and Diet Re-creation	35
What is a Wild UV Index?	45
What is the D3 Cycle and Effective Supplementation?	49
Chronic Kidney Disease in Reptiles and Hydration	57
The Light and Shade Method	63
Solar Powered or Solar Regulated?	69
Fitting Tips and Lamp Safety	77
Light-Sensitive and Albino Animals	87
Uv and Planted Enclosures	91
Amphibians and The Correct	
Provision of UV Systems	95
Conclusion	99
Glossary of Terms	101
Further Reading	107
Thanks And Acknowledgments	113

www.arcadia-reptile.com

The **Arcadia Guide** to MBD and its **elimination** in captivity

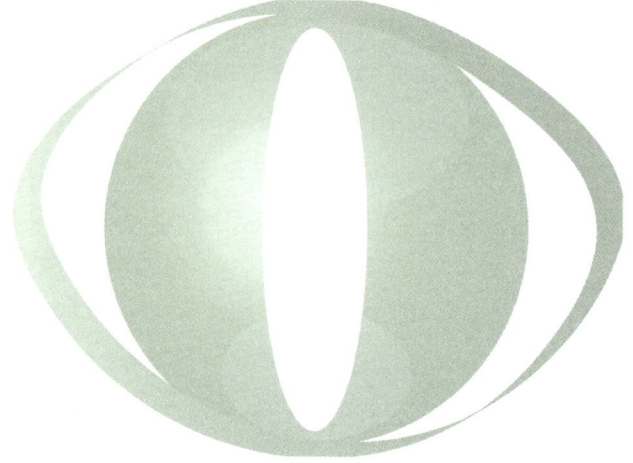

The **Arcadia Guide** to MBD and its **elimination** in captivity

FOREWORD

by David Alderton,
Editor, Practical Reptile Keeping magazine.

Back in the 1970s, when I was a veterinary student working at a practice in Sussex, we often used to have young turtles brought in as patients. They were frequently suffering from what was described back then as 'soft shell'. These poor creatures not only had an abnormally soft and rubbery shell texture, but they were often too weak to swim any more. There was sadly little that could be done to assist their recovery directly however, particularly if they came in during the winter months.

Those seen in the summer - especially a hot one like that of 1976 - did have a chance though, if their owners were prepared to place their pets in a sheltered and sunny spot outdoors each day, bringing them in at night. The turtles needed an aqua-terrarium, with shallow water and a rock where they could emerge and sunbathe, benefitting from the sun's ultraviolet (UV) rays. Lacing their food with a calcium supplement also assisted their recovery too.

While the source of the problem was known, there was little else that could be done. Why? There simply weren't the sophisticated lighting systems that are now available for reptiles to protect against what has become generally known as metabolic bone disease (MBD). Nature itself provided the only realistic - and slim - hope of a cure.

What saddens me greatly is that MBD still exists today. Rather like smallpox, it is an illness that should have been consigned to history. We know the causes of MBD and have the means to prevent it without any difficulty, as part of a standard husbandry routine nowadays.

I feel so strongly about this, having seen families distraught by the loss of their pets over 35 ago when there was little that could be done, to be in a situation today where, simply through lack of knowledge, not just turtles of course, but lizards and other reptiles are still suffering and dying from MBD. It can also afflict amphibians too.

The **Arcadia Guide** to MBD and its **elimination** in captivity

I am therefore delighted to see this highly practical guide, written with the aim of eliminating MBD. Spread the word to other reptile and amphibian keepers, particularly people new to the hobby, and let's help to banish this totally preventable and distressing condition without further delay.

David Alderton,
Author and editor of
Practical Reptile Keeping magazine
www.practicalreptilekeeping.co.uk

The **Arcadia Guide** to MBD and its **elimination** in captivity

The **Arcadia Guide** to MBD and its **elimination** in captivity

MBD AND ITS EFFECTS UPON CAPTIVE REPTILES

Introduction

MBD (Metabolic Bone Disease) is a term that makes every modern reptile keeper shudder. This condition is a large-scale killer of captive reptiles around the world and everyone that keeps reptiles indoors has the same chance that they may encounter the condition and its related symptoms. A simple online search of these three letters will return around 57,000 entries and some simply shocking images. What is MBD and what can be done to stop its progression through herpetoculture and can we ever find a permanent solution to these fundamental husbandry issues? The following guide lays

The **Arcadia Guide** to MBD and its **elimination** in captivity

out some modern thinking regarding the keeping of and the wild habitats of reptiles and seeks to find a way to "Eliminate MBD from captive reptiles". This must therefore be as part of a dedicated programme of care that takes into consideration living space, heat and light, UVA and UVB (ultra violet A and ultraviolet B), cool and shade and of course, effective varied diets, which is then topped up with targeted and safe supplementation. A policy of recreating wild exposure levels of heat, light, UV, humidity and diet must therefore be the only way forward for modern reptile keepers.

This advice is given after taking advice from vets and researching the wild behaviour and ecosystems of the wild species over a number of years. This information can then be crossed with the limitations of UV and heat systems in an aim to recreate these wild environments. Every keeper should, as part of the correct implementation of these ideas, undertake their own research as laid out in this guide so that the right system is chosen and maintained for the species that is to be kept and in the size of enclosure that is to be provided. This guide is not in any way purporting to take over from good veterinary care, your specialist herptile vet should be consulted at every point of suspicion of disease or an undersupply or oversupply of Ca/D3. This guide does however seek to provide keepers with the tools required to stop animals having to tolerate an undersupply over a period of time, and as such, we should see MBD become "Eradicated" over this period. We, as keepers, are becoming more and more knowledgeable about the species that we keep, and with this knowledge comes a marked improvement in the care that we can offer them. For us, the mantra of "Prevention is better than cure" is the standard by which we should all seek to live.

The fact that MBD (Metabolic Bone Disease) even exists in captive collections is evidence enough that we still have much to learn about reptiles and their effective care!"

With the increase of interest in keeping pet reptiles comes a pro rata increase of potential animal health limitations and problems. These problems could be with regard to animal selection, habitat maintenance and making the right choice of and how to make use of the now huge array of associated

The **Arcadia Guide** to MBD and its **elimination** in captivity

dry goods that are required to keep these animals fit and healthy. Our goal should always be to allow a captive animal to have the ability to thrive in captivity and not just expect it to survive.

Fortunately, reptile keepers are now far more educated about these animal groups than ever before and with the large-scale use of the Internet, much of this information can be shared and learned with and from each other at the strike of a key. Good scientific data, care sheets and shared personal experience via the forums are all good sources of some very valid information through at home and in the field observations.

Many of the old issues surrounding the proper maintenance of thermal gradients and even the correct identification of animals are now becoming a thing of the past but some very worrying issues still remain. MBD is a crippling and totally avoidable condition that has become a feared watchword in every collection. All captive reptiles are capable of suffering from the disease in its varying forms and guises but some species seem particularly prone to advanced cases of the disease. Crested geckos and water dragons, bearded dragons,

The Arcadia Guide to MBD and its elimination in captivity

chameleons, tortoises, many diurnal snakes and amphibia and controversially in some circles, crepuscular species like leopard geckos all present with the condition very regularly now. But why? What causes this disease and what can we all do proactively as keepers to limit the risk of an animal developing this disorder and its attributed conditions?

"Crested gecko with signs of advanced MBD courtesy of Rosie Reid, Wiltshire Geckos"

MBD facts.

MBD is caused by a largely unbalanced, unnatural (non-wild-like) diet in conjunction with an underpowered or ill-fitted UV system. A system that has all or part of these shortfalls would go on to produce not only a dietary shortfall but could also,

The **Arcadia Guide** to MBD and its **elimination** in captivity

over time, seriously inhibit the animal's ability to assimilate and utilise these compounds. This, along with a potential non-wild UV index over a period of time and alongside an ineffective thermogradient does indeed increase the risk of MBD and its related conditions. It is also clear that animals that are routinely given dietary supplements alone containing D3 are still able to suffer from MBD and the associated conditions.

It is extremely difficult if not impossible to recreate a truly wild diet with all of the food groups consumed by wild reptiles around the world. We simply do not have access to the correct information or even access to these food sources or information as to the ratio of consumption of these food sources per species. For example, we now know that the Bosc's monitor (*Varanus exanthematicus*) seems to consume a large amount of scorpions, wild carrion, wild succulents and small finch eggs in its wild range; to be able to recreate this would be almost impossible and undoubtedly unethical in captivity. Much work is still required to source and captively breed other live food sources for captive reptiles and amphibians in high enough numbers. The recent large-scale addition of fruit beetle grubs, butter worms, calciworms and silk worms among a few other grubs and worms has effectively opened up a new method of feeding wild grub eaters like mountain horned dragons (*Acanthosaurus crucigera*), water dragons (*Physignathus cocincinus*) and Calotes (*Calotes sp*) alike. I sincerely believe that we will start to see better captive breeding results with these species in the future as a result of this improvement (we just need to effectively recreate honeydew now for Phelsuma and their like).

- **MBD can present with a multitude of symptoms**, some of which are also very similar to an over-provision of synthetic supplements. Upon discovery, all of the individual symptoms should be checked by a good reptile specialist vet. The signs of potential MBD are varied and can include swollen limbs, lumps and bumps, fractures, chronic tiredness, soft shell, pyramiding in Chelonia, tremors and muscle cramps, non-feeding, fitting, nerve damage, zigzagged tails, shedding issues and paralysis. These are just some of the visible symptoms of the condition that is generally known as MBD. Just one of these symptoms on its own would be troublesome but when multiple indications of disease appear, the animal's biology is attacked and

The **Arcadia Guide** to MBD and its **elimination** in captivity

affected at every level. At the end stages of disease, the animal's bones start to become rubbery after releasing the bones' Ca reserves back into the bloodstream, and start to become swollen, bendable and can even break. The animal's mouth tends to become sore and will have greatly reduced movement, which can then progress on to a condition commonly known as rubber jaw syndrome. It is also common to see infected teeth (stomatitis) in animals with MBD. This condition has been linked to a reduced immunity due to a lack of both available vitamin D3 and vitamin A. Vitamin A deficiency has very similar symptoms to that of a critical lack of D3.

The animal groups that tend to suffer with this complaint are those herbivores on a restricted captive diet and those animals that have a high egg and crustacean content in the wild diet. Most of the species of anole (*Anolis carolinensis/ Sagrei*) for example, seem to be capable of suffering with infected teeth and infected eyes and repository infections, and I believe that this is due to a shortfall of hard-shelled crustaceans and small eggs in the captive environment.

Rubber jaw however is a terrible and largely incurable condition that presents with the animal's lower jaw losing its power of bite and alignment. It is common to see a shrinking of either the top or bottom jaw giving the animal an undershot or overshot jaw line. Rubber jaw can also, in extreme cases, cause the bottom jaw to bend midway along and present as a fully broken jaw. This obviously stops the animal being able to actively feed and obtain nutrients properly and so the disease completes with an early death, from starvation. Chronic tiredness also limits the animal's ability to hunt and feed, although some studies show that even late treatment for MBD will increase energy levels, which in turn, will increase the feeding response.

Chronic tiredness, if left untreated, will reduce the animal's ability to hunt and aggressively feed. Chronic tiredness may also reduce the animal's willingness to seek out and use the thermal gradients of the enclosure in which it lives, regardless of how ineffective they may be. Many animals that have been moved on to an effective HO T5 system display increased activity, brighter colours and a much greater feeding response rapidly after inclusion.

This then provides more energy for the animal to use and as such, increases the animal's ability to self regulate properly and go on to complete and use the D3 cycle. The full completion of the D3 cycle then allows good Ca and P absorption into the animal's body and the health and well-being of the animal will start to improve.

The Tremors that are associated with MBD are a very visible sign of disease and any animal that presents with shaking or even mild tremors must be taken for professional help as soon as possible. Neurological changes can become apparent with unusual (new) "star gazing" and even slight shaking. Another advanced warning sign is the loss of "Sticky feet" in climbing geckos like the day geckos (*Phelsuma sp*) tokay geckos (*Gecko gecko*) and crested geckos (*Rhacodactylus ciliatus*) among others. Advanced MBD seems to limit the efficacy of the hair-like setae on the soles of the feet and will stop the animal being able to climb properly throughout its enclosure.

Crested geckos are one species that seem very prone to acute and rapidly advancing MBD and can show advanced signs very quickly, even after early diagnosis. This, in reality, is not surprising when you look at the wild environment in which they live and now thrive. Occurring over areas of the Ile des pins in New Caledonia, which is a pine-forested island in the Pacific Ocean, they have access to a natural but huge UV index and a wide choice of prey sources over much of the year. In fact, the average weather information from Ile des pins weather station shows very high humidity and upper range temperatures close to 30°C in the height of the hot season. The local information also states that these islands only have two definite seasons, hot and humid and hot and stormy. The stormy season obviously hampers the index available to the animal and in this period the gecko would rely on a low UV exposure and the reserves that it had built up inside its body in the higher index seasons. On average, though, these animals live in an environment that provides them with access to a midday UV index topping 6–9, even if they do not use it in full strength, for much of the year. This densely forested environment would enable the animal to make full use of its ability to self regulate through movement and climbing to change its elevation in order to obtain stronger doses in short time spans through its sensitive skin, thus starting and completing the D3 cycle.

The crested gecko is a real triumph of international captive breeding; the species was thought to be totally extinct for a long time. Then, after a storm on Isle of Pines, a few individuals were rediscovered and brought into safety to be reproduced from. It is from these rediscovered individuals that all of the current captive stock originates. The fact that they have done so well to date with minimal care just shows what may be achieved under a fully energised system that allows them to self regulate as in nature.

Lumps are a visible early warning signal that something may be amiss with an animal. These lumps tend, in my experience, to appear quickly around the rear flanks and around the base of the tail. They are usually quite firm and also generally quite round in appearance. Obviously all lumps must be presented for professional veterinary diagnosis and should not be left untreated. These lumps are usually present alongside new kinks or waves along the tail and if this is so, it could be a strong indication of the start of a deficiency in the animal.

Mild or stop/start twitching and shaking are further warnings. This could be an unnatural shaking of the tail or slight vibration of the toes right up to extreme head wobbling. These symptoms must be out of the ordinary and not usual to your animal. For instance, many leopard geckos have a feeding response while hunting of waving the tail and some colour morph animals will have a natural tendency to star gaze or twirl. The enigma form of the leopard gecko (*Eublepharis macularius*) and the morph known as the spider royal/ball python (*Python regius*) are all well documented to display these genetic traits. If an unnatural or unusual pattern of behaviour becomes apparent then a vet's advice should be sought quickly and acted upon.

The mental state of the animal can be affected by long-term MBD or even an oversupply of synthetic supplements. A degree of stability seems usual after the blood chemistry is rectified. Heart and liver issues are usually present at the end stages of the disease and external symptoms of these

The **Arcadia Guide** to MBD and its **elimination** in captivity

conditions are hard to quantify and diagnose. Blood must be taken and a specialist vet's advice followed rigorously.

- **MBD is totally preventable in almost all cases**; the only real exceptions are with those animals that are born with the first stages of the disease or have been imported, after inadequate storage, from a third party. This condition should however stop occurring if future generations of parent animals are protected from an undersupply of D3 as well as being provided with a good diet and then given the ability to absorb these food sources. Exporters/farmers should also be incentivised to store and care for animals ethically. All reptiles and birds are capable of developing this condition but fortunately, it is not certain that they will go on to do so. This condition is very unstable and unpredictable and some animals seem to live long and apparently very healthy lives with minimal care. This is, however, the exception to the rule.

MBD is the result of a critical imbalance of Ca, D3 and phosphorus in the animal's body over a long period of time. This imbalance causes a chemical reaction in the animal's body which releases stored Ca back into the bloodstream and so causes a depletion of the animal's bone reserves. The prolonged lack of D3 then starts to reduce the animal's ability to absorb Ca back into the bones and bloodstream. In short, it can be likened to the old adage of "Two steps forward, three back". Bones can then become soft and misshapen.

MBD can also leave the muscles' ability to contract weakened until very little movement can be maintained, and this also applies to the muscles around the heart and lungs. This, coupled with chronic fatigue is a double-sided attack on the animal's ability to continue to self regulate and feed. Very lethargic animals may require assisted feeding and/or vet hospital care to get it on the mend and well again. Taking Ca from the animal's internal reserves is nature's way of protecting the animal's body from short-term shortfalls in the wild. If the Ca levels fall to critical levels, chemicals and hormones are released into the animal's body that cause these Ca reserves to be sent from the bones back into the blood stream for short-term re-use. This is in an attempt to protect the general and long-term muscle health and blood flow of the animal. It is also likely that the animal would also seek to protect itself in the wild in these darker, colder periods by entering brumation or even full hibernation. Brumation is a slowing down of the animal's system with regard to feeding and general activity without having to hibernate fully. Reptiles seem to be able to sense the seasons and enter brumation in good time to allow protection against harsh impending conditions. This also seems to affect captive animals that also react to the weather in the country in which they now live. Usually in nature the animal would then emerge out of this undersupply of D3 and Ca by entering the times of plenty and the wide dietary variety of spring and summer and the Ca/D3 balance would therefore be stabilised and rectified, leaving no lasting physiological or psychological damage. In captive surroundings, however, where the depletion is apparent over long periods if not for life, the Ca, phosphorous and D3 levels rarely balance and the depletion of the bone reserves carries on until the skeletal mass of the animal is negatively affected and eventually permanently altered.

The **Arcadia Guide** to MBD and its **elimination** in captivity

There are also numerous other effects throughout both the body and mental health and well-being of the animal. MBD causes weakened muscle contraction throughout the body and is found to be most problematic in the heart; this can lead to heart failure in the end stage cases. Advanced MBD also affects the ability of the animal's blood to clot properly, leaving the animal unable to repair damage to its body.

Nature's ability to protect a wild animal from a seasonal under supply has become the animal's worst nightmare in captive surroundings, when an unbalanced system is used over a long period of time perpetuating a release of stored calcium from the bones back into the blood."

- **MBD is now also thought to be extremely painful for reptiles, amphibians and birds**. MBD would be very similar to advanced rickets in humans. In fact, a critical lack of D3 in the human diet is also attributed to osteoporosis and other bone and nerve conditions, like Parkinson's disease, similar to those in reptilian MBD. Much more study is required to be certain of the extent of nerve damage through an undersupply or oversupply of D3 and Ca.

The most worrying thing about MBD is that it can be affecting the animal for a very long time before the symptoms first start to become apparent to the keeper as an underlying condition. It is in this period that the most positive measures can be included to address the advancing disease. Without a visible external change, most, if not all, keepers will be totally unaware of the disease as it progresses. However, small changes in the behaviour of an animal could be an indicator of internal changes and should be followed up with blood work and X-ray. Slight changes in the speed of movement or small tremors and "star gazing" are all early warning signs. Most keepers know their animals intimately and will have a general feeling that things are changing. These are the early warning signs for every keeper and specialist veterinary care should be sought to eliminate all possible chance of the effects of depletion.

- **MBD is not yet totally curable but we can now help some animals hugely.** D3 boosting, using high-potency UVB lamps and synthetic vitamin compounds and also calcium gluconate injections are now commonly used to help/halt the disease's progress. Damage to the animal's skeleton cannot be repaired completely but with the provision of a balanced dietary source and effective UVB systems, alongside painkillers in some instances, we can offer the animal a much better quality of life. We must, however, make changes to the long-term husbandry of the animal to be sure that an undersupply does not occur again. Human painkillers should never be offered to animals as this leads to death in most cases. Please consult your vet and follow his or her advice. If they feel that pain relief is required, they will prescribe the right medication in the right dose that will not harm the animal but allow it to live a more pain-free life.

- **One of the biggest causes of MBD is a lack of resource, reptile husbandry education and old-fashioned thinking on the part of both keepers and traders alike.** The

The **Arcadia Guide** to MBD and its **elimination** in captivity

common saying of "they don't 100% need UV" is very detrimental to whole animal groups. We have already shown how crepuscular animals can utilise sunlight in low indexes and in short time spans to still fully benefit from the D3 cycle in the wild. One example would be the crested gecko living in New Caledonia and using a thin, absorbent skin. This species lives in a forest that has an abundance of leaf scatter illumination. The animal is then able to self regulate throughout its habitat to find the strength of light shaft that it requires at that particular time.

Let's not forget that UVB is still available in measurable levels even in the most shaded of forests. If it is bright enough to see, it is bright enough to have a measurable and re-creatable amount of UVB. In essence, these thinner skinned animals could still hideaway out of the sight of many predators and just position part of the body in a shaft of natural sunlight. This column of light will have the same effect in the animal over time as full body basking but without undue risk of predation.

A mid-range T8 (5-6 per cent UVB) lamp, fitted without a reflector, at 15" from the animal would be recreating a level of UVB similar to the understory of these pine forests where these animals occur. We must keep in mind that many keepers use taller vivaria as is fitting for arboreal species. A lamp and reflector system of a higher power is therefore required to push the required index down on to the usual living space. UVB decreases in power the further that it has to travel from the lamp so the power available will be in a decreasing pattern downwards throughout the enclosure. The animal can then self regulate from high indexes at the top of the enclosure right down to shade style readings at the mid to low points. A balanced and well thought out system that provides a good thermogradient from hot to cool and a photogradient that matches light and shade is an essential part of modern captive reptile husbandry and is an essential element to the D3 cycle.

We can then start to look at recreating the average wild UV index of the chosen species in captivity. If a captive reptile has access to heat and cool, light and shade, wild levels of

UVA and UVB and has a full and balanced diet, the chances of going on to develop MBD drop dramatically. It should also be pointed out that reptiles do require a period of total darkness every day so light sources must be switched off for the night time period. If crepuscular activity is required to be viewed, then a good LED moonlight source can be used for a couple of hours at dusk into night and then again at dawn, if required. A good moonlight LED source would emit light around 460–480nm and produce no more than about 3–4 lux to recreate crepuscular light levels.

- **Young animals are particularly problematic.** Young animals grow quickly and do not have the potential built-up reserves of an adult animal. It is essential that the Ca/D3 provision for these young animals is balanced and in good supply. A young animal with a shortfall of D3 will not be able to absorb Ca properly but the animal will continue to grow and release Ca from the bones as the process of continued growth dictates. In short, whatever is invested into the animal in the young years will be paid out positively or negatively as the animal grows. It is also entirely probable that adult animals can only pass on the Ca that is available to them to the young, whether via egg or live birth. This is why we believe that the incidence of very young animals and animals at birth/hatching with the first signs of Ca imbalance appears to be increasing.

- **MBD should always be diagnosed by a good vet** and treated methodically with the clinician's recommendations. The longer depletion is left untreated, the greater the permanent damage will be. X-rays are essential along with blood work for a full and final diagnosis and should be allowed.

It is always a good idea, where possible, to remove an animal with diagnosed MBD from any community enclosure. It is far easier to regulate and maintain medication doses and dietary supplementation if there is only one subject to care for in an enclosure. Female animals that show signs of MBD or have a vet-diagnosed shortfall should not be bred from. Not only does the production of eggs or live young take a huge toll on the animal but the young may be more prone to deficiencies

The **Arcadia Guide** to MBD and its **elimination** in captivity

from birth. Some animals will continue to lay eggs even if not housed with a male. Both chameleons and bearded dragons commonly show this behaviour. If this is apparent in your animal, veterinary advice must be taken. Ca and D3 must be available to the animal at all times alongside an efficient and well-placed lighting system.

 *Providing enough energy from light and a full and varied diet as close to the wild animals is key to success!"*

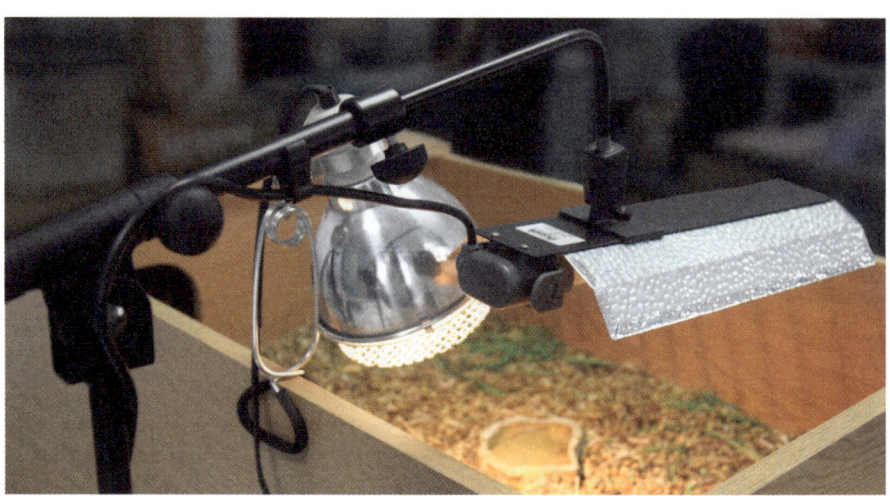

www.arcadia-reptile.com

DIET AND DIET RE-CREATION

Many keepers are breeding lots of species of roach now (*Blatptica dubia*) for example. These insects are excellent at supplementing the captive diet of larger animals and if you produce them at home you will know, without doubt, what these prey sources have been fed with. The disadvantage of in-home roach production is that they do breed very effectively and escapees can quickly become a problem in the home.

Many forms of fruit and vegetable are available in local supermarkets, markets and green grocers. A quick online search of wild plants and vegetative matter will help you find green foods that are likely to be consumed in the wild diet. Some of these plants and their flowers can be propagated in the home

The **Arcadia Guide** to MBD and its **elimination** in captivity

with great success and would be a very useful dietary addition to many species. A small hydroponic system can be used in the home with excellent results and is a great way of always having fresh fruit and vegetables available to your animals and if you grow your own, you will know what the plants have been fed on and treated with. This method would also allow the keeper to grow more exotic plants from seed that may be found and consumed in the country of origin but may not be available commercially grown in the keeper's locality.

Many insect eaters actually have a requirement for green foods and flowers, especially when young; look at the wild diet of the red headed Agama (*Agama Agama*) and Madagascan Iguana (*Oplurus cuvieri*) as an example, where succulents and flowers make up a proportion of the young wild diet. Variety is the key to the effective feeding of captive reptiles. We can then start to think seriously about providing effective heat and light gradients and how these gradients could be used to their full potential inside our enclosures.

We must endeavour to find out just how effective our own systems are; this could be from published brand data, independent testing sites or the use of handheld meters and thermometers.

A solar meter is a hand-held device that measures the differing wavelengths of light. At the press of a button, the keeper will not only be able to see how powerful the system is but they will also be able to use these meters to set and adjust light gradients and to recreate leaf scatter/rock scatter light patterns. The two meters that are most useful are the solar meter 6.2, which measures UVB in microwatts per cm squared (uw/cm2) and the solar meter 6.5, which measures the total index of UV provided (UVI).

You will notice that online weather stations list UV emissions per country as this index reading, and this can then be used to accurately recreate a basking area from the actual habitat of each species. We obviously cannot capture the sun and install it inside our enclosures. We can, however, through good weather station research, average out the wild UV index found in these wild habitats. We can then use this published data alongside the "light and shade method" to recreate a wild level of exposure relatively accurately by using the right power and type of UVB-emitting lamps. These systems will then be providing the animal with the very best chance possible of being able to be fully energised and to make full use of all of the dietary provision that has been offered throughout the day.

Another emerging thought is that those reptile species that have a predominant vegetarian diet also require more access to naturally sourced vitamin D3, produced through the natural UVB D3 cycle. Plant matter only really offers vitamin D2 so these species have become more reliant upon the sun to provide all of the vitamin D3 that they require. It is also now thought that these groups do not absorb D3 supplements well through the stomach, which can, over time, lead to a shortfall, even if supplements, used as assimilation through dietary sources does seem to be limited.

A variety of well-researched plants that may provide essential trace elements and dietary variance should be offered to more species than currently is the norm. Nyjer seed is found over much of Asia and Africa and is very oil- and Ca-rich, for example. These seeds could be of great use as a supplementary seed to Uromastyx lizards.

Lots of "apparent" insect only feeders will gladly consume small amounts of fallen fruits, green foods and flowers. In the wild, these plants would add in trace elements and minerals that may not necessarily be found with an insect-only diet. Many plants from Africa, for example, are rich in essential vitamins A and E and may make up a small but useful percentage of many ground-dwelling Agamids and of course, Chelonia. Some of the east African plants also have very high levels of Ca in their leaves and tubers; it is entirely possible that ingested ground nutrients (obtained from soil while feeding) and Ca made available from these plants could help to make up the full quotas required by the animal in its wild state.

A simple search of the tortoise care websites provides many lists of plants that are proven safe and those that should be used with caution or not at all. We could then start to look at using these wild plants to gut load our live food offerings and to then offer these to our animals. The bearded dragon (*Pogona vitticeps*) is a great example of a very commonly kept lizard that eats a variety of live foods and plant matter in the wild and in captivity.

The **Arcadia Guide** to MBD and its **elimination** in captivity

> " *There are no published accounts to date of any truly wild animals showing signs of visible MDB or the any of the conditions relating to an under or over supply of vitamin D3."*

All of the following food sources are now readily available. This clearly shows why Calci worms are so valuable as a food source. The ideal Ca:P ratio is thought to be 1.54

Table 1.*

Species	% Moisture	% Fat	% Protein	Ca:P Ratio
Mealworm	68.0	8.5	18.9	0.05
Morio Worm	59.8	15.2	19.5	0.10
Wax worm	65.1	15.5	15.5	0.19
Locust	73.2	5.8	15.9	0.19
Brown Cricket	70.7	4.4	19.8	0.32
Dubia Roaches	61.18	6.75	35.60	0.20
Calci worms	65.0	9.4	17.30	1.52

* Table 1. Supplied by Peregrine Livefoods.

These results were found from an online search. Butter worms have a very high ratio and should only be fed in moderation.

Species	% Moisture	% Fat	% Protein	Ca:P Ratio
Butter worm	58.54	5.21	16.20	2.1
Silk worm	76.0	10.0	64.0	Thought to be double of calciworm

- We should look to utilise, properly and safely, good quality, effective and measured dietary supplementation to make up some of the expected dietary shortfalls. The effective gut loading of live prey sources is essential in providing the animal with a food source that is packed full of goodness, however, we must keep in mind that whatever the insect is fed with is in turn fed to the reptile. If a single food source is fed as a gut loader to an insect over a short period of time that will be the only food source available to the reptile from the insect apart from the body of the prey source itself. A mix of food sources of both green leaves and root vegetables and fruits and a high protein source, similar to tropical fish flake food in moderation, is a good way of providing dietary variety to the insect. Good gut loading will also help to keep these insects well hydrated, which will also prolong the life of the insect and you should see less waste per box. It is worth pointing out that you can now obtain ready mixed gut loading diets from within the reptile industry. These mixes contain essential hydration, proteins and minerals. You should, however, research these diets before relying on them as a sole source of gut loading. Some of them appear to consist entirely of bran, which is of very little use as a gut loading agent in the long-term. A prey source should be fully gut loaded before being offered as feed to the animal. The inclusion of good supplements containing Ca should be used alongside an effective gradient of heat and light including UVB and a drop off into cool and shade as part of the D3 cycle. This will ensure that the animal has every chance of thriving and not just surviving in captivity.

Supplements should, however, be used with care and with regard to the guidelines set out by the brand that is chosen. If you are unsure of how much of a supplement to use or how to apply it properly or even the best way of storing the compounds, I suggest calling the brand owners to obtain the right information.

It is thought that supplements containing Ca and D3 start to break down very quickly after mixing. This could mean that the potency of some ready-mixed supplements reduces over time. It is thought that supplements that are hand mixed at the point of feeding could be much more effective as the active compounds have not had a chance to decline in efficacy.

It is now possible to obtain very effective shakeable tubs in which the insects and powders are placed at the point of feeding. This ensures an even covering of powder per insect and greatly reduces powder waste as it is easier to just mix up and use what is required for that particular feed.

The **Arcadia Guide** to MBD and its **elimination** in captivity

WHAT IS A WILD UV INDEX?

A wild type UV index simply means the average total index of UV as stated by the local weather stations in the country and/or location of the wild origin of each species. Animals in the wild will have the opportunity to move around the locality and self regulate their own exposure in these environments; indeed, many species have developed thin skins to make the most of lower light levels or with a quick foray into the leaf/rock scatter columns of light as they carry out their daily business. These animals still use UVB in the same way as their harder/thicker-skinned desert cousins but the reduction in skin thickness allows them to complete this process in a fraction of the time. At the other end of the spectrum, there are those animals that have developed built-in protection from the sun to help them live in high-index

The **Arcadia Guide** to MBD and its **elimination** in captivity

environments and to make the most of their place in the local ecology. The bearded dragon and the chuckwalla are both excellent examples of animals with a very thick skin that offers protection from harmful overexposure to the sun over long periods of time in the deserts in which they live.

The green iguana (*Iguana iguana*) is another example, this is a big brash animal that occurs in the tall trees and bushes of central and South America. This large lizard is a vegetarian and as such is not able to obtain much in the way of dietary Ca and D3 from the plants and flowers that it commonly eats. It has, however, developed an amazing ability to spend long periods of time high in the trees and in full sun. The green iguana has developed a skin that has differing degrees of protection from the sun in different parts of its body. The tail, for instance, which would be hanging down the branches and trunks of these trees and bushes is mottled brown in colour and offers almost total protection from the sun but the body that is coloured green and therefore hidden by the plants' foliage is much more able to absorb UVB. This means that the animal can spend the day foraging out of the view of predators and still benefit fully from exposure to the sun.

So does this mean that iguanas do not require high-level access to UVB or that they need a lesser percentage of UVB in captivity? The answer has to be a definite No. We must provide more energy at source to the animal to bypass the protection that nature has enabled it with so that it can experience a wild index and then go on to complete the D3 cycle as nature intended. Both of the animal groups, fully diurnal and crepuscular, use the sun in the same way but the thinner-skinned animals are able to use this exposure in a greatly reduced time span. It has been suggested that the skin of a bearded dragon offers 14 times more protection from the sun when compared with a leopard gecko. Does this mean that the leopard gecko does not require exposure? Certainly not! It simply means that it would take 14 times less time to achieve the same end result. There are some very interesting skin transmission results published at www.uvguide.co.uk.

The **Arcadia Guide** to MBD and its **elimination** in captivity

WHAT IS THE D3 CYCLE AND EFFECTIVE SUPPLEMENTATION?

This amazing process begins when a cholesterol called pro vitamin D (7DHC) is produced in the animal's skin (it is a natural process in humans too). When this cholesterol is exposed to natural light (including light in the UVB wavelength (290-315nm), it is turned into pre vitamin D in the skin membrane.

After exposure to warmth, this newly manufactured pre vitamin D is converted (in the skin membrane) into vitamin D3. It is essential to have this heating up period alongside UV radiation. Vitamin D3 is then sent out into the blood plasma and is bound with a vitamin D-binding protein. This is then carried to the liver where this part of this vitamin is converted to a hormone called calcediol (25-hydroxy vitamin D3).

The blood carries this calcediol all around the body and into the kidneys, where some of the hormone is turned into another hormone, called calcetriol. This compound then plays an essential role in calcium metabolism and controls the levels of calcium in the blood. Calcetriol also plays a huge role in the immune system and the cardiovascular system. It has been shown to lower the risk of cancers in the body and skin.

So we can see that exposure to natural sunlight is only the start of this amazing ability in reptiles, and humans alike, to turn sunlight into life-saving vitamins. This D3 cycle is dependent on the completion of the D3 cycle. If part of the cycle is missed out then the cycle cannot be completed properly. Changes and reactions would also be unable to be completed properly. This would result in an under-provision of essential vitamins and hormones, and if supplementation were not used, a calcium crash could happen.

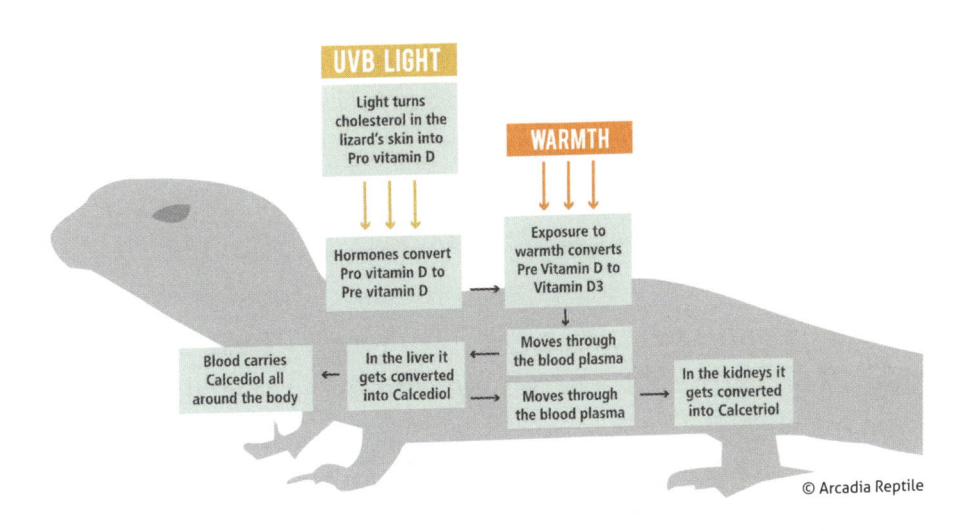

*The **Arcadia Guide** to MBD and its **elimination** in captivity*

UVB LIGHT — Light turns cholesterol in the lizard's skin into Pro vitamin D

WARMTH

Hormones convert Pro vitamin D to Pre vitamin D

Exposure to warmth converts Pre Vitamin D to Vitamin D3

Moves through the blood plasma

In the liver it gets converted into Calcediol

Moves through the blood plasma

Blood carries Calcediol all around the body

In the kidneys it gets converted into Calcetriol

© Arcadia Reptile

The risks of over supplementing.

Good quality supplements should always be offered but they cannot be passed through the system in the same way that D3 derived from UVB can. They can build up and can lead to potentially fatal conditions. Both hypercalcaemia and hypocalcaemia are a very real risk to the animal with haphazard and unmeasured supplementation.

What is Hypervitaminosis D? This is a toxic over-provision of dietary vitamin D. This becomes an issue as synthetics

The **Arcadia Guide** to MBD and its **elimination** in captivity

are not processed and then passed through the body as D3 gained from sunlight or UVB lamps is. The over-provision simply allows the over absorption of Ca "Hypercalcaemia" and all of the related issues of that condition. Early over-provision may present with the following symptoms: constipation, lack of appetite, chronic tiredness, muscle weakness and/or vomiting are all common. These symptoms that affect reptiles are very similar to those that also affect humans with the same condition. If you feel that your animal may be suffering from a toxic build-up of dietary D3, then you should consult a vet and ask for blood work to be done. In its early stages the condition is simply treated by discontinuing the use of any product with added D3 until the blood levels are again in the normal range.

What is hypercalcaemia? Hypercalcaemia is caused by an over-provision and absorption of Ca. This can be from feeding food sources that are dusted too heavily, too often with synthetic compounds containing D3, or even feeding live or meat sources to reptiles that are totally vegetarian in the wild. It is a very bad idea to allow chuckwallas (*Sauromalus ater*) for example, to eat non-vegetarian food sources. Hypercalcaemia causes defects in bones, heart conditions, physical shock, kidney damage, liver degradation and can also lead to fully developed liver failure. Defects that become visible in the bones and heart issues usually only manifest after it is too late; animals are adept at hiding these conditions as is dictated by the rule of survival of the fittest in the wild.

The only way to avoid hypercalcaemia is to regulate vitamin D3 supplementation and follow strict usage guidelines. The most effective and safest way to provide vitamin D3 is via natural unfiltered sunlight or a properly set up and effective solar recreation system. There are other risks and consequences to over-supplementation and the policy of use must always be as "supplementary". We should not rely on the sole use of synthetics to replace what millennia of natural selection has created. There certainly is no risk of over-provision through quality UVB sources that are provided in the correct way and making use of the light and shade method.

If you believe that your animal may be suffering from an overdose, cease usage immediately and consult a vet as a matter of urgency. The vet should be able to make a formal diagnosis, after blood testing, and will advise on the action that is required.

What is hypocalcaemia? Hypocalcaemia is an extreme and critical reduction of calcium in the animal's body. This can sometimes be referred to as the disease MBD itself. I believe that it is more accurate to class any reduction of Ca over a set period of time as hypocalcaemia, which, if left untreated, becomes chronic and then manifests as the condition that we now call MBD. Hypocalcaemia, if discovered, may be the diagnosis that helps the keeper to adjust the husbandry of that species and thus avert a short-term shortfall carrying on and becoming a fully developed case of MBD.

As in all aspects of captive reptile care we are all seeking to find total equilibrium between D3 provision phosphorus and Ca intake and effective assimilation. This can be maintained through a targeted and effective photogradient and a varied diet, which is topped up and monitored with good quality supplementation. We must, however, always keep in mind the tolerances and abilities to assimilate synthetic compounds of each species and adjust our offerings accordingly.

The main area of debate surrounding supplements is how to establish the correct dosage per feed and per species and of course the weight of the animal or animals in question. It cannot be correct that a reptile is fed the same quantity of supplement in relation to its size as to another species.

The quantity of powder used on an iguana's salad could, in actuality, be the same as the amount used on a water dragon's insects; these animals obviously differ greatly in size and diet so which dose is the correct dose? Is one over dosed and one correctly dosed or even under dosed? Does the fact that the iguana, being a herbivore and as such unable to assimilate D3 well through the diet, mean that it would need more or less powder? It is therefore advised that reptile keepers obtain exact information of dosage per species and per weight of animal from the brand chosen. If the brand cannot provide these details, it is advised that a different brand that is able to provide these essential details is researched and used.

CHRONIC KIDNEY DISEASE IN REPTILES AND HYDRATION

Kidney disease is another cause of quickly advancing MBD in captive reptiles. Many of the hormones and chemical agents required to make full use of the D3 cycle are produced in the kidneys of these animals, including calcetriol. The causes of kidney disease are numerous: from genetic defects right through to long-term dehydration or even injury. If the kidneys are unable to function properly and play their part in the D3 cycle, the cycle simply cannot complete and the body will release Ca back into the bloodstream, which will then be passed back through the body via its urates. The symptoms of kidney disease are very similar to MBD, with chronic tiredness and lack of interest in self regulation and feeding. If caught in the very early stages, this condition can be managed with medication and the progress of potential advancing MBD halted before it has had the chance to become a problem. It is essential that all reptiles are well hydrated according to the levels experienced in the wild. It is better, in the captive environment, to use good filtered water that is free of many of the chemical additions made to human tap water; we simply do not know the effect of these chemicals on reptile biology. Veterinary care is required even if there is a suspicion of this disease. Radiographs and ultrasound will be required for diagnosis of these conditions and should be insisted upon if you cannot get access to a specialist reptile vet.

One of the biggest causes of dehydration in captive reptiles is not providing these essential fluids in a way that the animals can readily make use of, for instance, species like the water dragon, mountain horned dragon and the day geckos commonly obtain fluids from rainwater and collected humidity which runs as water droplets down the leaves and branches in the forests in which they live. These species are simply not shaped well for drinking from a bowl and find it much easier to hang on the side of a branch and lap water as it travels downwards towards the forest floor.

It is essential that all forest species are sprayed daily so that the animal has the opportunity to obtain fluids and keep fully hydrated in this way. Automated spraying and misting systems can be a very valuable tool in ensuring that captive reptiles are kept hydrated. It is far more common for chameleons to be sprayed down daily as this information is commonly accepted and given by breeders and dealers. A well-hydrated reptile is able to flush through its system the impurities and mineral build-ups that may lead to infection and/or kidney damage and in doing so, help to protect the animal from developing MBD.

The **Arcadia Guide** to MBD and its **elimination** in captivity

High Powered UV lamps and strong supplements.

> *Ca powders should be offered all of the time! Ca+ D3 should be limited if high power lamps are used. Always check with the manufacturer to be sure of current guidelines of use."*

With the invention of much more effective and more powerful UVB-emitting lamps and the continued progress in making ever stronger supplements does indeed come a potential oversupply issue. If a wild UV index is being provided alongside the light and shade method, the animal's requirement for synthetic dietary D3 reduces markedly. Ca should always be provided but supplements containing D3 should be limited to the brand's recommendations. Most keepers who have had great success with a full index system only use compounds containing D3 every other week. These systems, when run alongside a full and varied and well gut loaded diet, will dramatically improve the animal's ability to make use of the foods that it consumes and offer the best protection against MBD and its associated conditions.

- "The pathway of light through the canopy and into the understory and finally in small quantities down onto the forest floor is unstoppable and perpetual".
- The leaves which make up the bulk of this canopy are able to reflect light in all directions and down on to one another. It is in this way that light is redistributed into the bulk of the forest. This light will work its way all the way down to the forest floor in decreasing amounts as it travels. It is worth noting that a large number of these scatter pattern light rays will be reflecting an almost full basking quantity of UV. Reptiles would be able to sit in these leaf flecks with a small amount of the skin in exposure and still benefit from the inclusion of natural UV energy "

The **Arcadia Guide** to MBD and its **elimination** in captivity

THE LIGHT AND SHADE METHOD

The light and shade method of lighting modern vivaria is a far more exact and effective way of providing light and energy from light to captive reptiles and amphibians. This method relies on the assumption that a wild type UV index can be effectively recreated and utilised after good research has been undertaken into the wild animal.

The Arcadia Reptile "Lighting Guide" has a huge amount of data, taken from weather sources, of average indexes and also shows exactly which systems are required to recreate this environment according to vivarium height. The light and shade method is very simple to set up and easy to maintain after exact research has been completed. The method is simply the division of an enclosure into a set hot and cool

The **Arcadia Guide** to MBD and its **elimination** in captivity

section as is normal with all reptile-keeping systems. The hot end then becomes the area that is washed with quality, upper index light to match the heat. Simply choose a lighting system that lights roughly a half to two-thirds of the enclosure. For example, a 34" 39w lamp would be used in a 48" enclosure. The lamp separates could be: UVFlood or slimline fitting or hybrid between T5 and D3 basking lamps or PureSunPro Halide systems, which would then be offset into the hot end so that the hot area is bathed in full-strength light and energy from this light. This energy from light then decreases in power as the animal travels into the cool and therefore shaded areas of the enclosure.

Cool and shade is as essential to the D3 cycle as heat and sustained UV. Hides and branches, rock work and live plants can then be situated from the hot end into the cool end, thereby allowing good self-regulation by the animal. Typically, an animal will positively self regulate in the hot end first thing in the day as it will seek to reach its target temperature quickly; and as in nature when basking in the sun, there will also be upper indexes of UV available to the animal as and when it self regulates. The animal will then, upon reaching its target temperature, carry on with its daily business of eating, drinking and hunting throughout the enclosure and regulate its own heat and light exposure accordingly.

We can set an upper index by providing rocks and branches high into the hot zone so that the animal can lift its elevation towards the lamp and in doing so obtain a higher dose. When decorating the enclosure, the elevation decreases towards the cool zone as in doing so the available index reduces accordingly. By providing these areas of high UV index and in contrast caves and hides at the resting shaded areas, we allow the animal to perform as it would in the wild and display wild self-regulation.

Allowing the animal to properly self regulate between a wild UV index and wild thermal gradient into cool and shade is ESSENTIAL to the D3 cycle and is KEY to the "Eliminate MBD programme". Reptiles, birds and amphibians are known to be tetrachromatic; this is the addition of a fourth cone-shaped cell inside the animal's eye that effectively opens up a whole new world of colour to the animal. Trichromates, like humans, can see around 1 million colours but not deep blues into UV or high reds into infrared, whereas tetrachromates can see far into the blue spectrum, including UV and infrared, adding up to a reported 100 million different colours. This ability allows them to see UV and its power gradients. They are then able to choose where to situate themselves to make the most of this exposure as and when they require it. It also allows them to find food easily as it is now thought that not only insects have fluorescent markers on them which would allow a predator to find them in dense foliage but the same applies to some plants and flowers. For instance, it is thought that iguanas see their favourite yellow flowers as bright day glow red, which would indeed help a large herbivore find a hidden food source in much the same way.

It has already been shown how urine trials left by rodents are seen by tetrachromates when exposed to UVA; this is a real bonus to those species that hunt live rodents as they will be able to see the trails left by the animals in the same way as some birds of prey can. Tetrachromacy is also thought to help with mate selection, especially in the monomorphic species. It seems that reptiles and birds not only display fluorescent patches that are invisible to trichromates but they know how to use them to attract a mate and warn off a rival. There is much more to learn about tetrachromacy at www.arcadia-reptile.com

Parietal eye

Much more research is required into the parietal eye that is found on the top of the head of most reptiles. This is not a blinking, fully functional, coloured eye but it does serve to help with thermoregulation and is surprisingly well developed in most species. For instance, the animal will be able to use the eye to detect cloud movement or predation from above and then move themselves into stronger or weaker areas of sunlight. This ability to sense shapes from above would also help in avoiding attack from above.

It is also thought that providing a high enough amount of light (LUX) is critical to the animal producing serotonin in the brain, among other hormones. This, among other factors, would help with setting breeding cycles as the days become longer and brighter or to set laying periods for accurate gestation and incubation. The parietal eye is a very important and largely undiscovered part of reptile biology that will unlock many secrets to captive care in the years to come.

The Arcadia Guide to MBD and its elimination in captivity

The Light and Shade Method

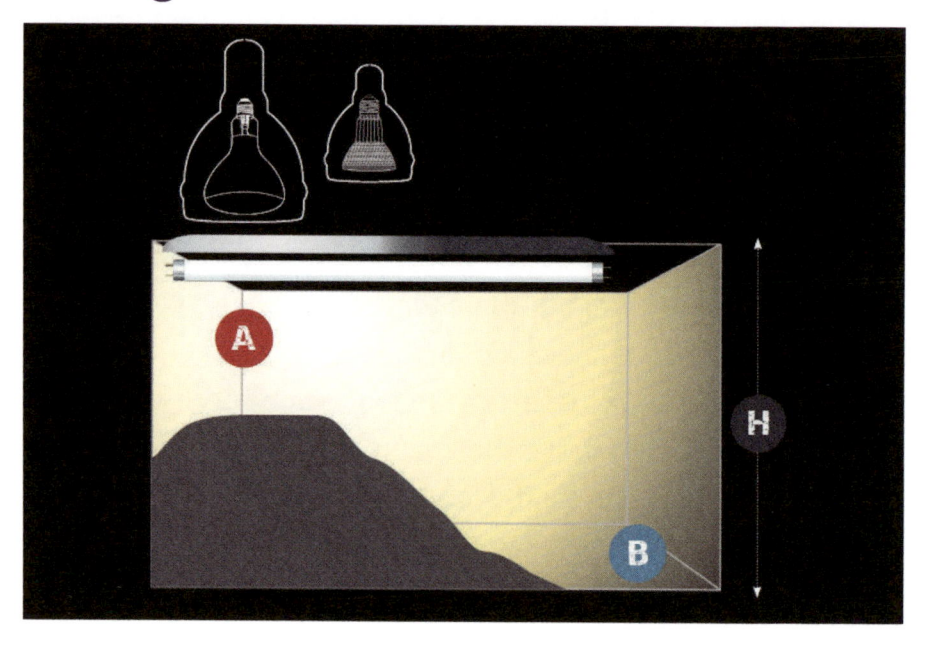

SOLAR POWERED OR SOLAR REGULATED?

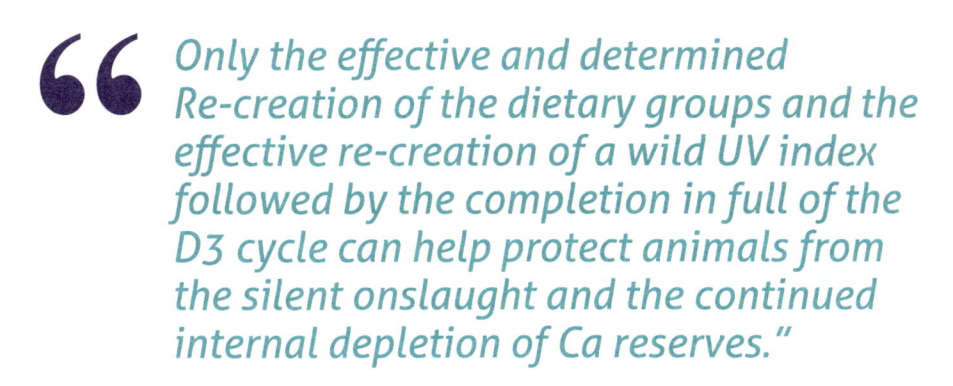

> *" Only the effective and determined Re-creation of the dietary groups and the effective re-creation of a wild UV index followed by the completion in full of the D3 cycle can help protect animals from the silent onslaught and the continued internal depletion of Ca reserves."*

Reptiles are described as ectothermic (cold blooded); this simply means that they need to obtain heat and therefore energy from an external heat source, i.e. the sun, in the wild

The **Arcadia Guide** to MBD and its **elimination** in captivity

or an artificial heat source in captivity. They do not use food to create heat and energy within themselves in the same ways as endothermic (warm blooded) species, including humans, do. This ability has many positive aspects for survival in the wild. In times of plenty when food sources should be more abundant, the ambient temperatures will be high enough for the animal to obtain energy and make use of these feeding and breeding seasons. In times of scarcity, the animal's requirement for food would reduce as the temperatures available through these darker, colder times reduce. The animal is in effect protecting itself by slowing down its behaviour and using less of its fat reserves, thus sustaining itself during the colder months. This does however mean that these animals do require an external source of heat to survive.

The only real source of heat to wild reptiles all over the world is the sun, whether this is from direct exposure or from heat that has built up over the day. We have all seen film of various snakes and lizards apparently basking on the roads at the end of the day. It is in this way that they obtain heat from the road or rock that has built up during the day. This is good crepuscular behaviour, adapted to modern surroundings, using low light levels through thin skin to top up through the D3 cycle and obtaining heat in a safer lower light environment.

The sun provides heat and life-giving energy to the world. Part of this heat is visible and invisible light. Light is broken up into wavelengths, which are described as and measured in nanometres (nm). This graph commonly starts at the left of the chart which is called zero. This is known as X-Ray and moves up from there into visible and then again into infrared which is invisible light to humans.

The next wavelengths of note are at 260–280nm, which is termed, UVC. UVC is very short wavelength UV and destroys cells and organisms. It is not present on earth naturally as the earth's atmosphere blocks any radiation in these highly dangerous wavelengths.

UVC is used in hospitals to destroy pathogens; it is also used in most pond filtration to kill algae cells.

UVB is present on the earth in the hours of daylight and is the wavelength that most life forms, including humans, use to generate vitamin D3 inside their own bodies through the D3 cycle. We look for a peak in activity at 297nm for reptiles as this is the wavelength that is most effective in starting and maintaining the D3 cycle.

Then we have the wavelengths from 310–400nm which is termed, UVA. It is probable that the wavelengths in the low 300nm could also allow the production of some D3. This is termed short wavelength UVA, and as we approach 400nm, it is termed long wavelength UVA. It would be this wavelength that is used in nightclub black lights and is not useful for D3 production. UVA is, however, used in balanced quantities by reptiles and birds, primarily to "activate" their tetrachromatic vision.

Reptiles are able to see a vast array of colours, many more than humans can. In fact, it is thought that a human can only see around one million colours whereas tetrachromates are thought to be able to see and utilise around one hundred million colours. Reptiles being able to see UV would be able to move their position into these columns of light (leaf/rock scatter illumination) to obtain the specific dose that they require at that time. It is in this way that I believe crepuscular animals select power gradients in low light levels and are able to make full use of them.

Human vision starts at around 400nm which we perceive as deep blues. Then we work up through ever lightening blue and into green, yellow and then finally, as visible to humans, red. As we ascend further still up the graph, we enter infra-red which again is invisible to humans and is described as heat.

Light is provided to the earth by the sun and an irrefutable component of the sun is both UV and true infrared. So reptiles are able to rely upon the sun to provide them with heat from these infrared wavelengths, visible light for diurnal and crepuscular species and UV for the production of life-giving vitamins. If there is visible light in nature, there is UV! It does not matter how much light is blocked by the canopy of even the most densely planted forest; if you can see your hand in front of you, there will be measureable and therefore usable levels of ultraviolet light.

How many species are limited to life on the ground? Being able to see power gradients of light and having the ability to

The **Arcadia Guide** to MBD and its **elimination** in captivity

take from nature that which is required for life and coupled with the ability and inclination to climb, surely we can now see how the whole forest is used by wild animals. Reptiles have developed a requirement for external heat and as UV is part of this whole spectrum of light including heat, they have developed the ability to make full use of the wavelength. Even those species that are more active at night, like tree boas for instance, are still commonly found sleeping by day in the trees. A reptile does not have to be awake to benefit fully from the D3 cycle. These chemical and hormonal changes still happen in the body whether the animal is awake or asleep. Reptiles rely upon the sun and it is surely one of their greatest allies. The sun supplies them with energy from heat; it provides them with a miraculous visual ability that helps them to find food in dense forests.

Tetrachromacy is thought to be used in mate selection and for positioning in the environment to obtain the strength of light that they require as that time. Reptiles are also able to make full use of the D3 cycle so that they can assimilate and make full use of the nutrients that they have consumed during the day. Reptiles are truly reliant on the sun and upon the cycles of the sun for their whole pattern of life and survival. Even those truly nocturnal species are still reliant on the ambient heat that has been produced during the day and then released back from the rocks and hard surfaces.

Most true night–time active species are also found basking/sleeping in the open in the day or will use narrow columns of light on part of the body as they hide away. We can see the evidence of retics (*Python reticulatus*) found basking by day, white lipped pit vipers *(Trimeresurus albolabris)* and tree boas (*Corallus caninus*) curled in the trees and amphibians, like dart frogs (*Dendrobates sp*) or reed frogs (*Hyperolius sp*), tucked in the fronds of plants or in the long grasses, for example. All of them are obtaining life-enhancing energy from the sun and are truly "Energising" in readiness for the exertions of the impending night. So reptiles are truly solar powered and are able to make full use of "Solar Re-creation" in captivity if provided in the correct and measured way.

If we can understand the requirements of light per species and recreate these ecosystems, we will not only be offering the animal the very best possible chance of survival and reproduction but we will greatly reduce the risk of MBD developing and harming the animal at any stage of its life.

It must go without saying that "all of the secrets of great captive care are hidden in the wild animal" and by looking to nature, we will, without doubt, uncover important factors and systems that can be replicated in captivity for the ongoing benefit of herpetoculture.

The **Arcadia Guide** to MBD and its **elimination** in captivity

FITTING TIPS AND LAMP SAFETY

The invention of good quality UV lamps for reptiles and amphibians is, without doubt, the most important addition to reptile care in the home in recent years, during which time, these lamps have in general become better quality, with better colour and much more powerful. We have, over the years as keepers, been able to advise each other as to the best way of using these lamps and how to get the very best out of the systems that we offer our animals. Some of this advice has been very good and some has had serious consequences. For example, we must never lower lamps of any kind to eye level in an enclosure, especially those lamps that emit UV rays. The idea behind this old advice was correct in theory but in practice the animals are exposed to a very high risk from photo-kera-conjunctivitis (PKC). The thought

The **Arcadia Guide** to MBD and its **elimination** in captivity

was that as T8 lamps do not have a very big range of emission, we could increase the exposure available to the animal by lowering the lamp inside the enclosure.

Reptiles have been designed as a whole to be illuminated from the top down. This is why they have those hard, bony protruding eyebrows and the parietal eye. These eyebrows are in effect sunshades and offer protection against glare in the heat of the day. If a light source is placed inside an enclosure, side on to a reptile in an environment in which there is no real escape from this bright light source, the eye can become inflamed from the glare of this light source. This inflammation can then turn to an infection of the cornea and if left untreated, this infection has been shown to be able to spread throughout the animal. So the original idea that did make some sense on paper actually made a different and very serious condition worse.

The other reported cause of PKC in captive reptiles was with regard to the use of largely unbranded lamps that were shown not to have good protection from emissions of harmful UVC. This wavelength will very quickly damage the animal's eyes and also the animal as a whole and poses a huge risk to the keeper. It is vital that reptile keepers are sure of the output and quality of their brand of choice.

So what is the best way of providing light to reptiles?

Firstly, we must choose the right system for the species that is to be kept and for the size of enclosure in which it is to be kept. We should start by looking at the average wild exposure of the animal in question and its reported daily activity. For instance, we can very easily see from tourist reports and the parks department records that the bearded dragon is regularly exposed to high levels of light/UVB in the deserts in which it is found and is seen basking and feeding at high index times of the day without access to much tree cover, as is common in deserts.

These dragons usually have rock and burrow networks close by at all times to provide them with safety and also an area where shade and lower temperatures may be found. In contrast, we can see that the water dragon is able to seek

The **Arcadia Guide** to MBD and its **elimination** in captivity

out and use similar levels of light and UV but readily has the ability to self regulate this exposure throughout the heavily forested areas in which it is found. As keepers seeking to provide our animals with the very best, we should seek to recreate these gradients.

We then need to look at the output of the lamps that are available; only then will we be able to ascertain which lamp should be used to generate the output that is required. We then need to be sure of how much energy is produced by this lamp and over how wide an area and for how long. We can then use this information to set the index that is common to the wild animal at the basking space. The basking space is commonly 12–18 inches from the lamp. As already stated, UV decreases in power massively the further it has to travel from the lamp. So, the higher the enclosure, the more power is required at source to lower the required indexes down into the usual living points.

It is entirely possible that a High Output T5 D3+ or 12 per cent UVB reptile lamp could be used effectively and ethically with a leopard gecko. But this type of lamp would only ever be used with this species if the enclosure was high enough to provide the required index at the usual basking zone, which in the case of this species, would be close to the floor. It is far better to use rocks and branches in the basking zone to build up a layered environment for the animal to climb around and increase its own exposure level as required.

To make this process even easier, we have included a free and interactive lighting tool on our educational website entitled "The Lighting Guide" this will work out for you exactly the products that are required for your chosen species in your height enclosure. This feature can be found at www.arcadia-reptile.com

All lamps have inherent built-in design limitations and it is up to us as keepers to be fully aware of these limitations and alter the environments in which our animals live so that the animals can in turn obtain exactly the exposure that is required at that time. As stated previously, UV does not travel very far from the lamp itself. UV rays also naturally degrade in potency during the life of the lamp as the phosphors used in the lamp degrade. The longer a lamp is used, the weaker the

The **Arcadia Guide** to MBD and its **elimination** in captivity

output will become. It is essential that you know how effective your system is and when the lamp or lamps will need to be changed. Some lamps have been shown to only really be upper level effective for 3–6 months. The Arcadia Reptile brand is guaranteed to be upper strength potent for one whole year; this is based on a 10–12 hour a day photoperiod.

Please make sure that you accurately note the date that a lamp was included into your system so that you can make sure that this lamp is changed in good time and that your system remains potent at all times. Arcadia Reptile offers a FREE reminder service by email to help you with this. Reflectors are an essential addition to all lamps and massively increase the efficacy of UV systems both inside vivaria or external to a mesh top. Lamps, both linear and compact, emit light all of the way around the lamp, which means that up to two-thirds of the light and energy produced from this light can be wasted from this inherent limitation.

The use of a good reflector system will harness the total power of the lamp and push this light and energy from light down on to the living area where it is most required. A good reflector will at least double the amount of available energy to the animal and as such, will enable your system to become much more effective. Reflectors should be wiped monthly with a damp cloth to remove any dust particles and dried water deposits. They should also be changed when they become permanently scratched or misted. Typically, a good-quality reflector will last 2–4 years depending on the environment in which it is to be used.

For those enclosures where a mesh top is used and the lighting is placed on the outside of the enclosure, extra care must be taken. We can easily see from simple meter tests that a wire mesh can reduce the amount of light and energy from light available through the mesh to the animal by around 30–40 per cent from new. This limitation does vary slightly from brand to brand of enclosure. This reduction can be made even worse over time as the metal becomes rusted and dusty. It is good maintenance to remove these mesh tops for brush cleaning once a month to help with the provision of light and replace them yearly with new tops.

We have been able, at Arcadia Reptile, to design a very special dimpled reflector especially for these mesh-topped

The **Arcadia Guide** to MBD and its **elimination** in captivity

enclosures. These reflector systems are as standard in both the "viv top canopy" and the "UVFlood" and this type of reflector is over 20 per cent more effective at forcing light through a mesh than a plain polished reflector. These reflectors work by forcing light not only directly downwards but also side to side. This aids in pushing the light through the rectangular holes of the mesh.

Lamps need to be offered in the right position to be sure of their potency in your system and to ensure that they are offered in a safe way to the animal and keeper alike. Light must be provided from the top of the environment and, as is stated in the photogradient section, should be sited in the hot zone, leaving the cool zone in shade.

The right lamp holders also need to be chosen and where local laws apply, adhered to. There are two common types of lamp holder: IP64 or water resistant and IP67, also known as waterproof (Ultraseal). Lamps use electricity and it is vital that this is used with respect and in a safe manner. If you have a desert species with little to no humidity then the IP64 water resistant lamp holders can be safely used. If you have a humid or even wet environment, including spray and mist systems, then an IP67 (Ultraseal) lamp holder/controller must be used.

All of the Arcadia Reptile T5 products are complete with IP67 lamp holders as standard. Although these systems will be waterproof, it is important not to allow direct spraying of water on to the lamps as this poses a cracking issue with hot glass. The lamp can then be fitted ideally in the corner between the roof and the front plate of the enclosure, above the door. This then ensures that the light is provided above the animal, at the right angle and that the lamp is hidden from human view. In the case of mesh-topped enclosures, where lamps the full length of the enclosure are used, simply decide which is to be the shaded area – either the front or the back of the enclosure – and then place the canopy either in the front section or the back section.

Lamps must be sited carefully but firmly in the lamp holders so that a good contact between lamp pin and power source is supplied and maintained. If the lamp cap will not push on with moderate pressure, DO NOT force it but check that the pins are properly located in each hole in which they need to be seated. If the lamp is forced, the pins will bend or break

The **Arcadia Guide** to MBD and its **elimination** in captivity

and the lamp will be useless. Make sure that lamps are seated safely in the correct-sized lamp clips and that the lamp is secure and cannot be pulled down or sat upon by the animal. It is an excellent idea to use a quarter of an inch twill-weld wire to create a box section guard around the lamp inside enclosures where climbing animals are kept, especially those containing snakes as they love to coil around and sit on cooling lamps. This can then present as a burn risk when the lamp becomes hot again.

LIGHT-SENSITIVE AND ALBINO ANIMALS

Many people assume that lighting albino animals is not a good idea due to the reduced level of protection in their skin and their light-sensitive eyes. In reality, these animals are able to make full use of light and the energy from light in the same way as normal or non-albino morph animals can. Some keepers rely totally upon dietary supplementation with these red-eyed animals. We have been able to find a solution to providing the natural D3 cycle to these animals without causing distress. As previously stated, reptiles are able to adjust their own position around an environment either in the wild or in captivity in order to obtain the exposure that they require. We feel that if an animal is offered a targeted

The **Arcadia Guide** to MBD and its **elimination** in captivity

system with the opportunity to fully self regulate between exposure and shade, they will do so readily. We have seen leopard geckos with red eyes lie in an enclosure with their body exposed to light and their head hidden from this light in the mouth of a hide. Reptiles really are extremely clever. It is then up to the keeper to provide this light in the right way and in the right concentration and to match this light with suitable hiding spaces. For example, leopard geckos are now produced in an amazing array of colour mutations and many thousands are kept in homes all around the world.

These animals would still use light in much the same way as the wild animal does but due the reduced level of protection in the skin, it would seek out light in lower levels. If we provide a system that is around half the power/index of the system that would be used for the wild animal and provide caves and hides, the animal will self regulate throughout this environment and take energy from light as and when it needs to. The photoperiod can also be reduced to match the needs of the animal. From my point of view, I would rather provide a targeted zone of UV in these enclosures just for an hour or two a day than rely totally on synthetics. The animal will soon let you know how it feels through its behaviour. Very many of these morphs will bask in the light for 20 or 30 minutes in the open before going back to the cave and some of them will spend longer or shorter periods of time doing so. All we need to do is allow the animal to choose. Some very high mutations, including the enigma, may now be so light sensitive that a decision could be made not to provide any light at all. We must keep in mind the animal's needs at all times.

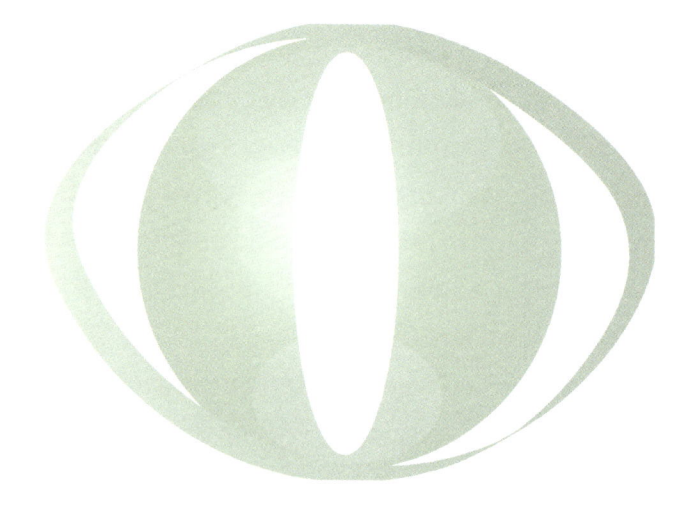

The **Arcadia Guide** to MBD and its **elimination** in captivity

UV AND PLANTED ENCLOSURES

Many reptile and amphibian keepers quite rightly now require their enclosures to be fully live planted. In the past, growing plants in an enclosed space and with the inclusion of high powered UV lamps has caused great problems with regard to leaf burn and eventual plant decay. It is vital that reptiles and amphibians are still able to obtain the exposure that they require to thrive in captivity. We can now provide and manage a system of care that does not damage plants as was common beforehand. Plants require the right amount of energy from light at the right wavelengths of light, water, airflow and foods to grow. If these elements are maintained, the plants will readily grow and flourish. Typically the waste from captive reptiles is a very good source of plant nutrition, and we simply need to

The **Arcadia Guide** to MBD and its **elimination** in captivity

make sure that there is good air flow in the enclosure, the right lighting and that the plants are well hydrated, generally from the roots up. Interestingly, bromeliads fair far better if they are wired on to a branch and are not planted into soil. They are then kept hydrated via spraying the leaves and core inside the enclosure.

The first thing to do is to set your solar recreation system; this is the part of the system that sustains the D3 cycle for the livestock. We can then start to think about adding in another lamp as part of a targeted hybrid system to help the plants grow inside the enclosure. Plants require certain wavelengths of light to grow and a high enough PAR (Photosynthetic Active Radiation) to cause the plants to sustain this growth. Just the inclusion of a second lamp will increase the PAR that is available to the plant; it is then the colour output of this second lamp that needs some thought.

There are many live planted enclosures that use a hybrid system of Arcadia Reptile D3 HO T5 lamps and a secondary plant growth lamp like the "Freshwater Pro" or the "Original Tropical Pro". Both of these lamps are true HO T5 in design and were designed to grow plants under water originally – this is why they are so effective at sustaining growth in a terrestrial system. We need to include and provide light in the blue and red wavelengths, which plants need to flourish. The Freshwater Pro will engineer an environment that has a crisp bright look and the original tropical pro has a deeper, slightly darker jungle feel. Both lamps will cause plants to grow and will not affect the livestock living in the enclosure. If all aspects of plant care can be maintained alongside the provision of the D3 cycle, there is no reason why these plants should not flourish alongside the other inhabitants of the enclosure.

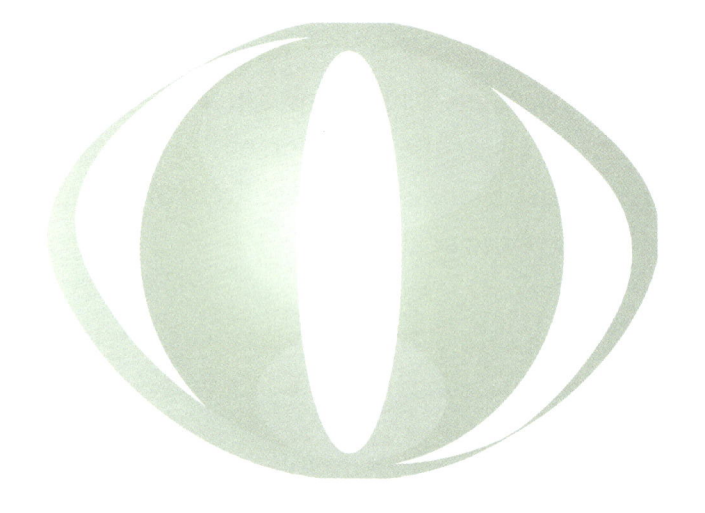

The **Arcadia Guide** to MBD and its **elimination** in captivity

AMPHIBIANS AND THE CORRECT PROVISION OF UV SYSTEMS

Terrestrial Amphibians are capable of suffering from a lack of absorbed Ca in much the same way as reptiles. Currently, more and more keepers and research facilities are finding and expanding on the links between the sun and terrestrial amphibians, including dart frogs. It does seem that even a slight reduction in absorbed Ca is able to be seen on an X-ray. One study indicates that a 15 per cent reduction in Ca is visible via X-ray. This marked reduction may be because of the very thin nature of frog bones. It is also now thought that the devastating explosion of chytrid fungus is partly due to a

The Arcadia Guide to MBD and its elimination in captivity

reduction of sunlight/heat and UV getting through the forest clouds which seem to be thickening due to global warming.

This seems to affect the species commonly found at higher altitudes more than those that are found on the true forest floor. The good news is as found through Andrew Grays' work at the Museum of Manchester and in situ in Costa Rica that when infected frogs are exposed to an elevated temperature and given a wild index of UV, the fungus simply dies off. Much more about this new development can be found on the Manchester Museum "Frog Blog" http://frogblogmanchester.com/2010/12/01/altered-states-altered-environments/

This evidence of certain species of amphibians using the sun in a much more intimate way than historically thought, does back up the in-home research that is going on all over the amphibian-keeping world. Care must be taken to only recreate a wild Index and to provide a natural habitat with plenty of areas of light and shade. As with all reptile keeping, the light and shade method is very important to the successful keeping of amphibians. Follow the wild indicators. If tadpoles are fully protected in the wild by being totally wrapped in leaves or hidden in caves or deep in moss, then exposure may not be of benefit but the adults should still be given the opportunity to seek out light if and when they require it, if they display this behaviour in the wild. Targeted emission zones through heavy live planting does seem to be a very effective way of providing this energy from light to captive amphibians, without the risk of over exposure.

As with all reptile and amphibian keeping the animals are the very best indicator of wellness. If your animals readily bask high in the enclosure you could add in a higher basking platform. If they seem to hide away all of the time less power could be used or extra shade provided.

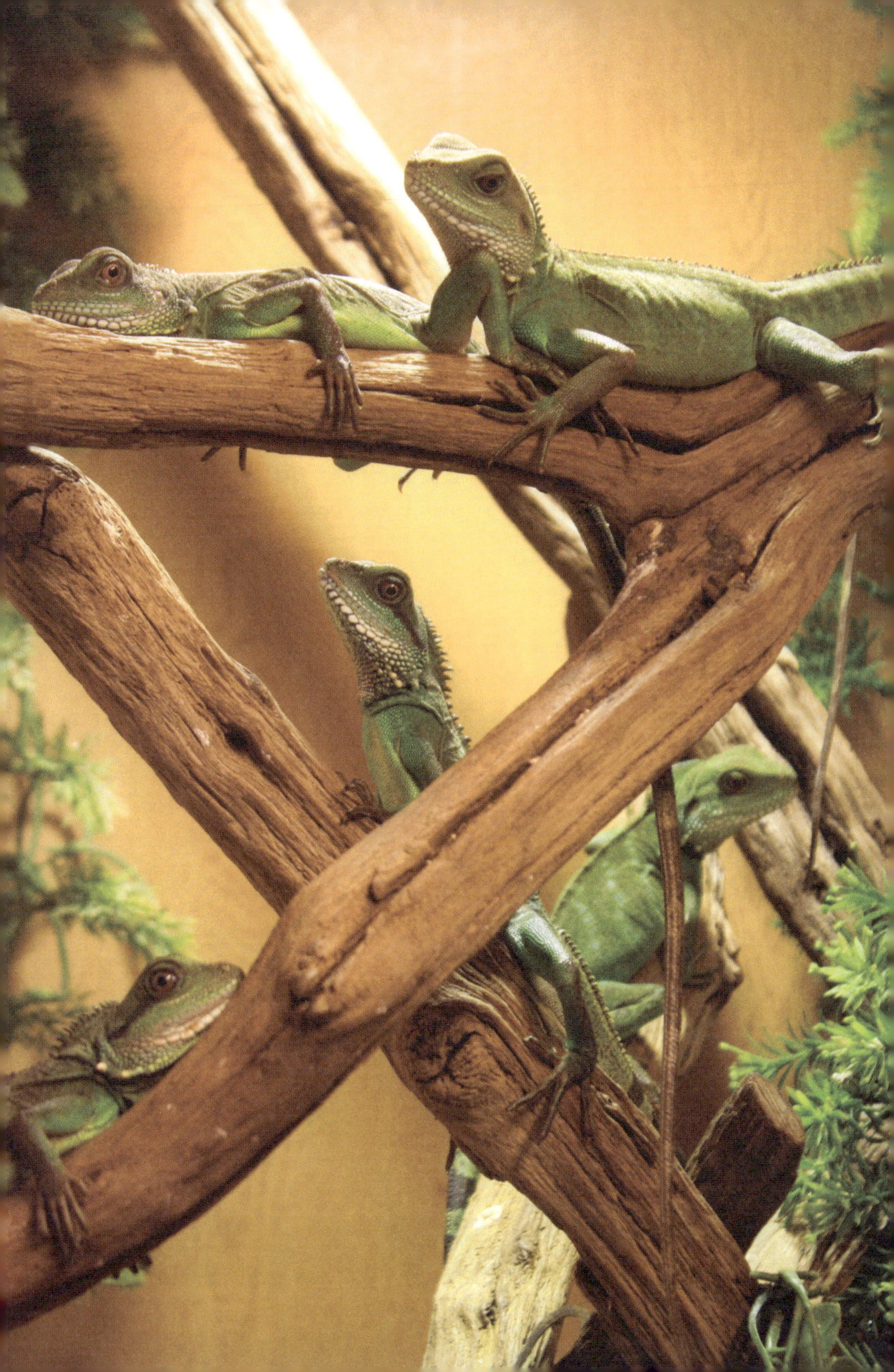

CONCLUSION

It is true to say that reptile keeping is more advanced now than it has ever been but we must all agree that there is still much more to learn. I believe that all of the secrets of great care are indeed hidden within the wild animal and in the environment in which it lives. Certain key indicators are available to us as keepers by way of small behavioural changes within our enclosures. It is up to us as ethical keepers to watch out for these indicators and to adjust our enclosures accordingly so that our animals have the best of care at all times.

> "Reptiles and amphibians are sometimes thought of as primitive, dull and dimwitted. In fact, of course, they can be lethally fast, spectacularly beautiful, surprisingly affectionate and very sophisticated."
>
> Sir David Attenborough, "Life in Cold Blood"

The **Arcadia Guide** to MBD and its **elimination** in captivity

The new solar recreation systems are the first step in a huge leap forward towards eliminating MBD in captive collections and if used correctly, we should all start to see very exciting results. Whatever happens along the way, reptiles will continue to enthral us all and provide many hours of enjoyment to like-minded people all over the world.

John Courteney-Smith ©

GLOSSARY OF TERMS

Ca; this is the chemical symbol for Calcium. This is the mineral responsible for building and maintaining healthy bones and maintaining a healthy blood supply.

Controller; this is the term used to describe the electronic or magnetic device that starts and runs fluorescent lamps.

Crepuscular; this is the term used to describe animals that are more commonly seen active at dawn and dusk. This behaviour may be because of the animal's sensitivity to light or as a long-term predator-avoidance measure.

D3 cycle; this is the term used to describe the cycle required by animals to produce and use vitamin D3 inside their own bodies after exposure to natural sunlight.

The **Arcadia Guide** to MBD and its **elimination** in captivity

D3; vitamin D3 is responsible for allowing the assimilation and use of calcium among many other important functions.

Gut loading; this is the term used to describe the practice of feeding insects that are to be used as live food before they are in turn fed to an animal.

Hybrid system; this is the term used to describe the use of a system where more than one lamp is used for a differing purpose. i.e. for live planted environments.

Thermogradient; this is the term used to describe a gradient of temperatures from hot at one side of an enclosure to cool at the other.

MBD (Metabolic Bone Disorder); this is a condition that affects captive animals via a depletion of calcium reserves from the bones.

Nocturnal; this is the term used to describe those animals that are only typically found active at night.

P; this is the chemical or periodic symbol for phosphorus

Photogradient; this is the term used to describe a gradient of bright light that is graduated into shade.

Photoperiod; this is the term used to describe the amount of hours a day that light is provided throughout an enclosure.

Reflector; this is a polished surface that has been designed to capture light from all the way around a lamp and focus this light back down into the enclosure.

Solar Re-Creation; this is the term used to describe a system of lighting that re-creates the level of exposure that an animal would be able to use in the wild.

Supplements; this is the term used to describe synthetic vitamin and mineral powders that can be added to an animal's diet to supplement dietary shortfalls of these important elements.

T8/HO T5; this is the term used to describe the diameter of a lamp. A T8 lamp is typically one inch (26mm) in diameter and is described as standard output. T5 is the term used to describe a lamp that is five-eighths of an inch (16mm) in diameter but is still described as standard output. Arcadia Reptile, however, pioneered the development of and only produce HO T5 reptile lamps. These are described as True High Output. These lamps use a high output electronic signal and high output phosphors. This means that these lamps emit 2–3 times more light and energy from light when compared to a T8 of a similar length and wattage.

Tetrachromacy; this is the term used to describe those animals that have four cone-shaped cells in the eye. This effectively allows these animals to see a whole array of colours that are invisible to trichromates like humans. Trichromates= 1 million colours; tetrachromates=100 million colours.

UV; is the term used to describe the wavelengths of light in the ultraviolet spectrum.

The **Arcadia Guide** to MBD and its **elimination** in captivity

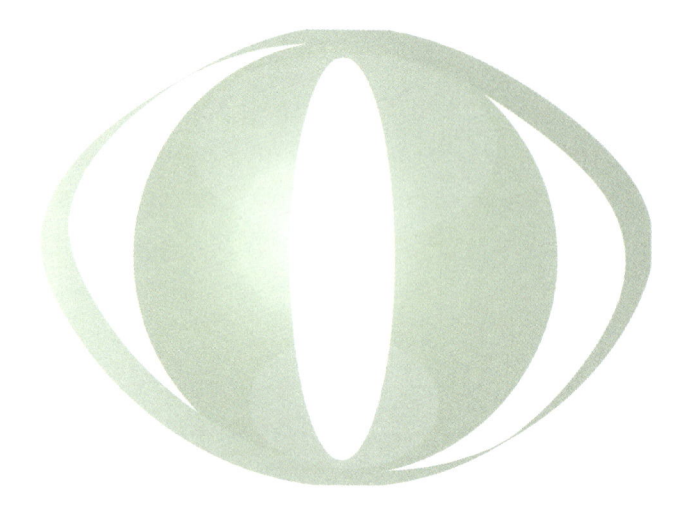

The **Arcadia Guide** to MBD and its **elimination** in captivity

FURTHER READING

Bernard, J.S. and D. E. Ullrey. 1995. An illuminating discussion of Vitamin D, U-V radiation & reptiles. 2nd Proc.Assoc.Rept & Amph.Vet: 40-42

www.reptileuvinfo.com/docs/ultraviolet-light-and-reptiles-amphibians.pdf ; Journal of herpetological medicine and surgery. "Ultraviolet light reptiles and Amphibians"

www.anapsid.org/iguana/bernard-d3.html ; Idiosyncrasies of Vitamin D Metabolism in the Green Iguana (Iguana iguana)

http://ajcn.nutrition.org/content/61/3/638S.long ; environmental factors that influence cutaneous production of vitamin D1-3

www.epda.eu.com/en/research-papers/2011/prd/01-01-prelatdisord/ ; Amelioration of osteoporosis and hypovitaminosis D by sunlight exposure in Parkinson's disease

www.rmki.kfki.hu/~lukacs/TETRACH.htm tetrachromacy

www.downloads.ircf.org/Iguana14_1%20Light%20and%20Reptillan%20Immunity.pdf ; aspects of light and reptile immunity

http://aris.ss.uci.edu/~kjameson/jamesonOUP3.pdf tetrachromatic colour vision

www.anapsid.org/stomatitis.html ; ulcerative stomatitis (mouthrot) in reptiles

http://elewa.org/Horticulture/VegetablesinEastAfrica.pdf ; Elewa, vegetables of east Africa

www.reptileuvinfo.com/docs/vitamin-d-house-geckos-texas-spiny.pdf ; Elliott N. Carman, Gary W. Ferguson,

William Gehrmann, H. Tai C. Chen, Michael F. Holick, and M. E. Douglas (2000) Photobiosynthetic Opportunity and Ability for UV-B Generated Vitamin D Synthesis in Free-Living House Geckos (Hemidactylus turcicus) and Texas Spiny Lizards (Sceloporus olivaceous). Copeia: January 2000, Vol. 2000, No. 1, pp. 245-250

www.sidneyanimalhospital.com/downloads/Caresheet_reptile_03_MetabolicBoneDisease.pdf ; Sidney animal hospital guide to MBD

www.greenigsociety.org/mbd.htm ; Green Iguana society guide to MBD

www.anapsid.org/diverskidney.html ; Clinician's Approach to Renal Disease in Lizards

www.veterinarypracticenews.com/vet-dept/avian-exotic-dept/nutritional-related-diseases-in-reptiles.aspx ; Nutritional Problems in Reptiles

The **Arcadia Guide** to MBD and its **elimination** in captivity

http://woodlandparkzblog.blogspot.co.uk/2012/01/ultra-awesome-ultraviolet-eyesight-in.html ; Ultra awesome: Ultraviolet eyesight in animals

http://users.jyu.fi/~hesasi/publications/PDF%20UV%20reviewOikos.pdf ; Ultraviolet vision and foraging in terrestrial vertebrates

http://wikis.lib.ncsu.edu/index.php/Sahm,_Crenshaw ; The Third Eye: Parietal Eye and Pineal Gland

www.justairplants.com/index.php?option=com_content&view=category&layout=blog&id=68&Itemid=94 ; Creating a planted vivarium

http://ajcn.nutrition.org/content/84/4/694.full.pdf+html ; The case against ergocalciferol (vitamin D2) as a vitamin supplement1

www.weatheronline.co.uk/weather/maps/forecastmaps?LANG=en&CONT=afri&UP=0&R=300 ; online global weather station.

www.youtube.com/watch?feature=player_embedded&v=hO6kNvd3hCA

http://news.bbc.co.uk/1/hi/sci/tech/7464437.stm

http://frogblogmanchester.com/2010/12/01/altered-states-altered-environments/

The **Arcadia Guide** to MBD and its **elimination** in captivity

THANKS AND ACKNOWLEDGMENTS

Firstly thanks must go to my parents for introducing me to the world of exotics and to my wife and son for putting up with all the weird and wonderful animals that find their way into our home. I would also like to thank Frances Baines for her constant guidance and support. Thanks must be pointed out to the Arcadia Reptile team for all the help and support shown while I was writing and a huge thanks to David Alderton for not only writing the forward but for his continued support through PRK. Thanks to Jamie and his team at Chameleoco for the use of the images and for your advice. And lastly thanks to everyone else that contributed in any way to the writing of this guide.

John

NOTES: